I.—FROM NECESSITY TO TRANSCENDENTALISM IN COLERIDGE

From his college days onward Coleridge considered himself, and was considered by his intimate friends, the champion of religion, and particularly of the Christian religion. That this championing of Christianity was frequently attested in his letters and writings; that the most ambitious poem of his youth—*Religious Musings*—was written in the spirit of its title; that he occasionally preached from Unitarian pulpits; that all his later prose writings were predominantly religious; that he at no time considered the writing of poetry his prime purpose—these facts lead to the conclusion that religion was the dominating interest throughout most of his life.

In Coleridge's religious history as reflected in his writings there are two broadly marked stages, divided at about the year 1798-9—the period of his visit to Germany. In the first stage he was a Necessitarian, and almost simultaneously a Unitarian, while in the second he became a

Transcendentalist. The changes in his mind, though rather radical, can be accounted for both historically and psychologically. All his writings that touch on religion, including *The Rime of the Ancient Mariner*, fall chronologically into their place, showing a natural sequence in his spiritual development. In the first period (1794-1798) the religious thought of the poet is governed chiefly by the conception that God, at the center of everything, predetermines and regulates all physical and mental life into a sort of universal harmony, or unity. Expressed as opinion in the earlier poems, this conception is sublimated into a pervasive spiritual atmosphere in *The Rime of the Ancient Mariner*.

I

NECESSITY AND UNITY

The poem *Religious Musings* was partially written in 1794, when Coleridge was twenty-two, and was completed and published in 1796. " I build my poetic pretensions on the *Religious Musings*," wrote Coleridge to his friend Thelwall at the time of its publication. The poem indeed represents a very serious effort; but it is important for what it intends to perform rather than for what it performs. Its style is turgid and grandiose; it has nothing of the simple, terse, idiomatic English which Coleridge achieved in his later poems. Though it has no great intrinsic literary value, it was often considered in Coleridge's day as his most important deliverance,[1] and is

---

[1] "I have read all your *Religious Musings* with uninterrupted feelings of profound admiration. You may safely rest your fame on it."—Charles Lamb, in a letter to Coleridge, 1796.

"I was reading your *Religious Musings* the other day, and sincerely I think it the noblest poem in the language next after the *Paradise Lost*."—Charles Lamb, in a letter to Coleridge, January 5, 1797.

-FROM NECESSITY TO TRANSCENDENTALISM IN COLERIDGE

By

S. F. GINGERICH

PR
4483
.G56
1965

828.7
G67G5

significant as indicating the trend of his most serious thinking at that period when his mind was in a formative state. Its thought, complicated and not wholly self-consistent, is dominated by the principles of Necessity and of Unity.

Necessitarianism, which is known as determinism in philosophy, is opposed to Free-will. "I am a complete necessitarian," Coleridge wrote to Southey at the time he was composing *Religious Musings,* "and believe the corporeality of *thought,* namely, that it is motion." In another letter of about the same time he speaks of himself as "a Unitarian Christian, and an advocate for the automatism of man." He thus conceived of mind as merely an automatic and passive instrument through which the cosmic order finds an avenue of expression.

Unitarianism says that God is all and that God is love. In a letter to John Thelwall in 1796, in which Coleridge incidentally affirmed that even from the point of view of poetic sublimity Isaiah and St. Paul and St. John easily surpass Homer and Virgil, he wrote: "Now the religion which Christ taught is simply, first, that there is an omnipresent Father of infinite power, wisdom, and goodness, in whom we all of us move and have our being; and secondly, that when we appear to man to die we do not utterly perish, but after this life shall continue to enjoy or suffer the consequences and natural effects of the habits we have formed here, whether good or evil. This is the Christian *religion,* and all of the Christian *religion.*" It is striking that in this passage, which makes the bold claim to express the whole of Christianity, there is not even so much as a hint of the orthodox idea that man is sinful and is saved by grace, and that whatever harshness lurks in the Calvinistic conception of Necessitarianism is immediately removed by the Unitarian conception that since God is love, all are elect and no human being can be given over to eternal punishment. With Necessity at one pole of his thought and Unity at the other the young poet felt he had solved the riddle of the universe and that he had a living message for the world. This message, he proudly remarked in one of his letters, was to be found in his literary works; it is indeed completely summed up in *Religious Musings*.

The principles of Unity and Necessity fairly jostle each other in rivalry for the first place in the reader's attention. As to Unity, the poet repeatedly suggests that " one Omnipresent Mind," whose " most holy name is Love," is diffused through all things; that in the " meek Saviour," " whose life was Love," is the only perfect revelation of the Godhead; and that when men are filled with this love they come to know themselves as " parts and portions of one wondrous whole." In one passage, for example, the poet speaks of the soul soaring to perfect Love,

>Attracted and absorbed: and centered there
>God only to behold, and know, and feel,
>Till by exclusive consciousness of God
>All self-annihilated it shall make
>God its Identity: God all in all!
>We and our Father one!

Just at this point, however, the idea of Unity is crowded out by that of Necessity, or Predestination; for the passage continues:

>And blest are they,
>Who in this fleshly World, the elect of Heaven,
>Their strong eye darting through the deeds of men,
>Adore with steadfast unpresuming gaze
>Him Nature's essence, mind, and energy!
>And gazing, trembling, patiently ascend
>Treading beneath their feet all visible things
>As steps, that upward to their Father's throne
>Lead gradual—else nor glorified nor loved.

" Thus from the Elect, regenerate through faith, pass the

dark passions," repeats the poet forty lines forward, and declares that the Predestined are "by supernal grace enrobed with Light, and naturalized in Heaven," becoming one with the Father, which is "the Messiah's destined victory." So the poet constantly passes from Unity to Necessity and back again, thus closely interweaving the two ideas in the poem.

Though the poem is speculative throughout, the poet aims to bring its philosophy to bear directly upon the religious, political, and social evils of the day; he attempts to "cope with the tempest's swell" of "these tumultuous times"; and he strikes with all the energy of undisciplined genius. He vigorously attacks the "Fiends of Superstition, that film the eye of Faith, hiding the present God," "diffused through all, that doth make all one whole"; the unbeliever is a sordid solitary thing.

> Feeling himself, his own low self the whole;
> When he by sacred sympathy might make
> The whole one Self!

The poet mentions a specific offence against this religion — the refusal, in January 1794, of the House of Lords to accept a proffered peace from the French Republic. His wrath was kindled against those who held that the sole purpose of the war upon the French was the preservation of the Christian Religion. To mingle fiendish deeds with blessedness, to defend the "meek Galilaean," with his "mild laws of Love unutterable," by the scourge of war and the prayer of hate seemed to him nothing short of blasphemy.

He rouses himself even to greater indignation against the social evils of the day—"the innumerable multitude of wrongs by man on man inflicted." He expresses sympathy for orphans and poverty-stricken children, aged women and poor widows, and men driven by want to deeds of blood—the wretched many "whom foul Oppression's ruffian gluttony drives from life's plenteous feast."

But in spite of this severe arraignment of all the wrongs committed by man, the poet is convinced that there will soon be a rapid regeneration of mankind, and that in fact all evil is but temporary in character and really the immediate source of greater good. Thus from avarice, luxury, and war, he asserts, sprang heavenly Science, and from Science Freedom. Even the oppressors of mankind are beneficent instruments of Truth—

> These, even these, in mercy didst thou form,
> Teachers of Good through Evil, by brief wrong
> Making Truth lovely.

Coleridge's evil thus turns out to be no evil at all, but only a dream. His sense of the world's wrong, entirely vague and theoretical, quickly gives way to the conception, so common in the last decades of the eighteenth century, that very shortly the human race shall be changed into a blessed brotherhood of man. Coleridge thus optimistically peoples the earth with "the vast family of Love," each heart self-governed yet each belonging to the kingdom of Christ, and all parts of the one Omnipresent Mind. "A Necessitarian, I cannot possibly disesteem a man for his religious or antireligious opinions—and as an *Optimist,* I feel diminish'd concern,"—so wrote Coleridge to Thelwall in 1796 in reference to *Religious Musings.* A true Necessitarian cannot blame a man for holding any given opinion, any more than he can blame a stone for lying where it lies—both positions being inevitable, and the one as remote from individual responsibility as the other. On the other hand, Coleridge's principle that God is all and is Love left no room in his scheme for the existence of evil, and he logically became an unqualified optimist. So the poet concludes as he began, breathing "the empyreal air of Love, omnific, omnipresent Love":

> Believe thou, O my soul,
> Life is a vision shadowy of Truth!
> And vice, and anguish, and the wormy grave,
> Shapes of a dream![2] The veiling clouds retire,
> And lo! the Throne of the redeeming God
> Forth flashing unimaginable day
> Wraps in one blaze earth, heaven, and deepest hell.

Though Necessity and Unity are thus the dominating ideas in the poem, they are not the only ones in it; for Coleridge's mind was, from the first, essentially eclectic. Since the poet drew material from diverse sources of his extraordinarily wide reading, fragmentary and obscure parts are not fused with the leading ideas, and contradictions appear. However, this is no more than is to be expected from a youth of high enthusiasms and of great susceptibilities, who has not yet thoroughly assimilated all his materials. But the poet takes care that the divergent parts are kept subordinate to the main ideas.

We may here ask from whence did the young Coleridge get the principles of Unity and Necessity? The answer in its main outlines can be given briefly. As to Necessity, aside from what of Calvinistic theories of Predestination came to him through the ordinary channels, he got his ideas directly from eighteenth-century philosophers, among whom may be named: Hartley, naturalist and associational philosopher, who emphasized the theory that thought is corporeal and is motion, and who treated the mind as an automaton; Priestly, scientist and theologian, who in theology taught the doctrine of philosophical necessity;

---

[2] "I thank you for these lines in the name of a necessarian and for what follows in next paragraph, in the name of a child of fancy."
—Charles Lamb, in a letter to Coleridge, June 10, 1796.

and Godwin, whose *Political Justice,* published in 1793, claimed to base all its reasonings on the principle of Necessity. Godwin's influence is especially noticeable in those parts of the poem that discuss the social and revolutionary problems of the day. In 1795 Coleridge addressed a sonnet to Godwin, in which he asserts it was his voice that

> Bade the bright form of Justice meet my way—
> And told me that her name was Happiness.

Besides, it must always be remembered that in the eighteenth century poets and philosophers and divines thought much more commonly in terms of Necessity than in the nineteenth; whereas in the nineteenth they thought much more commonly in terms of Free-will. Pope's " Whatever is, is right," was a popular expression of an oft-repeated conception of eighteenth-century philosophy; while perhaps the profoundest expression of determinism was Jonathan Edwards's book attacking the Freedom of the Will (1754), which Godwin quotes approvingly so far as it bears on philosophical Necessity. It is to be expected that when Coleridge was disciplining his " young noviciate thought in ministeries of heart-stirring song," as he says in the poem, he would show that he had drunk deep from the prevailing philosophy of the preceding generation.

As to Unity, aside from what he gathered from such idealists as Plato, Plotinus, and Berkeley, he got his Unitarian ideas directly from the Bible, particularly from the writings of St. John. In the poem, such phrases as " His most holy name is Love," " Him whose life was Love," " In whose sight all things are pure," " We and our Father one," and still others, are direct echoes of the Fourth Gospel.[3] In the notes, both those discarded from some of

---

[3] The early Unitarians were literalists in interpreting the Scriptures, and naturally held the Gospel of St. John in high esteem.

the earlier editions and those that were permanently retained, he also shows a close affinity in thought to the Book of Revelation.

In short, the poet attempted to harmonize his own interpretations of the Scriptures with the teachings of his favorite authors—philosophers and theologians. It was a magnificent effort, but unsuccessful—because of the inconceivability of any one's combining in a single scheme the philosophy of Plato and of St. John with that of eighteenth-century Materialists and Necessitarians. Yet the poet did achieve a certain harmony—satisfactory, it seems, to the people of his time — as, for example, to Charles Lamb—by blending the principles of Necessity and Unity.[4] Temperamentally Coleridge was easily in-

But later this Gospel grew in disfavor with them because it emphasizes the Divinity of Christ. Coleridge, however, never followed the Unitarians very closely, either in their early literalism, or in their rejection of the Divinity of Christ. He always retained a profound reverence for the Gospel of St. John. See the quotation near the end of this article from Notes on the Book of Common Prayer, also *Table Talk*, June 6, 1830: "It is delightful to think, that the beloved apostle was born a Plato," etc.

[4] Priestly made an almost identical combination of Necessity and Unity in his philosophy. A recent commentator, C. C. Everett, in *Immortality, and Other Essays*, says of him:—" His belief in necessity was simply an intense form of faith in God. Since everything was determined by God, what place is there for grief or anxiety? It was a marvel to his childlike mind that Calvinism, starting as it does from the thought of the sovereignty of God, could reach results so terrible. The sovereignty of God meant to him the sovereignty of a wise goodness. He believed that Calvinism thus carried at its heart a principle that would one day transform it into a system of beauty." It may be suspected but cannot be proved that Coleridge got his ideas ready-made from Priestly. First, there seems to be no direct evidence in the case. Secondly, it is well-nigh impossible to track Coleridge specifically in his borrowings, because of his subtly intermixing materials from various sources and of his interpenetrating them with something of his own. It appears he was only in general indebted to Priestly.

clined to try to reduce all things to one principle, to a Unity—that is, to see the One in the many. And while in emphasizing the principle of Necessity he was harking back to eighteenth-century ideas, in drawing upon the more ancient sources of the Bible and Plato for the mystical principle of Unity, and attempting to express it in terms of the emotions and the imagination, he anticipated the spirit of the nineteenth century, and so far became a prophet of what was to be.

In the brief poem *To A Friend,* written also in 1794, Coleridge asserts that nothing can be gained by prayer—an extreme form of Necessitarianism, since it presupposes that God has literally predetermined every detail of life:

> He knows (the Spirit that in secret sees,
> Of whose omniscient and all-spreading Love
> Aught to implore were impotence of mind) —

Likewise in *The Eolian Harp* (1795) he conceives universal life as automatous:

> And what if all of animated nature
> Be but organic harps diversely framed,
> That tremble into thought, as o'er them sweeps
> Plastic and vast, one intellectual breeze,
> At once the Soul of each, and God of all?

The fragmentary poem *The Destiny of Nations,* written in 1796, narrating the story of Joan of Arc, begins with a long invocation to "the Will, the Word, the Breath,—the Living God," who is "Infinite Love." It then lengthily explains that "the infinite myriads of self-conscious minds are one all conscious Spirit," and that if men fancy there be rebellious spirits in the Universe that arrogate to themselves power over dark realms, these still teach hope and yet "train up to God." For Fancy first unsensualizes the dark mind, giving it new delights and teaching self-control " till Superstition with unconscious hand seat Reason on her throne." Thus all things in the universe, including superstition, and evil itself, help, in a necessitarian spirit, to " evolve the process of eternal good."

In the story Joan did not act upon her own initiative, " for a mighty hand was upon her." She went forth alone,

> Urged by the indwelling angel-guide, that oft,
> With dim inexplicable sympathies
> Disquieting the heart, shapes out Man's course
> To the pre-doomed adventure.

At the close the poet also pre-dooms, not only all Enthusiasts, however wild-eyed, but all Prophets, each to their respective fates, and hymns the praise of God:

> All-conscious Presence of the Universe!
> Nature's vast ever-acting Energy!
> In will, in deed, Impulse of All to All! . . .
> Glory to Thee, Father of Earth and Heaven!

In the preface to the *Ode on the Departed Year* (1796) the poet asserts that " the Ode commences with an address to the Divine Providence, that regulates into one vast harmony all the events of time, however calamitous some of them appear to mortals."

Thus the principles of harmony, unity, and optimism, governed by the law of Necessity, furnish the chief intellectual matter of these poems (1794-1796). They are all somewhat abstractly conceived, and their religion may be said to be a religion of opinion rather than of experience.

But in later poems (1797-8) we see the abstract ideas gradually becoming humanized. This was the period of the poet's finding himself, of change and growth, and especially of the deepening of his spirit. The breaking down of the scheme of Pantisocracy, upon which Coleridge had for a time staked his future, a serious rupture with his most intimate friend, Southey, his marriage to Sarah Fricker—all of which events occurred in the latter part of 1795—his becoming father of children in 1796 and 1797, his ensuing struggles against serious financial difficulties, brought him rather suddenly face to face with actualities. His sense of responsibility for those dependent on him, which was strong during these years, wrought deeply on his naturally affectionate nature. It not only humanized, but simplified his religious outlook. Moreover, his acquaintance and ripening friendship with Wordsworth in 1796 and 1797 immensely quickened his intellectual powers, gave a profounder resonance to his emotional life, and deepened his sympathy for individual and concrete things in life and nature. As a result, the religious poems of 1797 and 1798 were born of personal experience rather than of abstract speculation. The same principles, as formerly, govern the poet's thought, but they are now rendered by suggestion, and are approached by some simple, deep-felt, personal emotion. The poems are just as religious in spirit, but not so obtrusively religious as the earlier ones. They show a more intimate touch with nature and a far finer sympathy with the concrete objects of nature. The abstract " God diffused through all " of the *Religious Musings* becomes in *Fears in Solitude* (1798) " All sweet sensations, all ennobling thoughts, all adoration of the God in nature," that keep " the heart awake to Love and Beauty "; or, as expressed in *This Lime-Tree Bower My Prison* (1797):

>   So my friend
> Struck with deep joy may stand, as I have stood,
> Silent with swimming sense; yea, gazing round
> On the wide landscape, gaze till all doth seem
> Less gross than bodily; and of such hues
> As veil the **Almighty Spirit**, when yet he makes
> Spirits perceive his presence.

It is to be noted especially in *Frost at Midnight* (1798) how from a very simple situation—himself and his cradled infant at the hearth-fire of his cottage—he rises without seeming effort through personal experience to a grand climax which expresses profoundly and religiously his conception of Unity:

> For I was reared
> In the great city, pent 'mid cloisters dim,
> And saw nought lovely but the sky and stars.
> But *thou*, my babe! shalt wander like a breeze
> By lakes and sandy shores, beneath the crags
> Of ancient mountain, and beneath the clouds,
> Which image in their bulk both lakes and shores
> And mountain crags: so shalt thou see and hear
> The lovely shapes and sounds intelligible
> Of that eternal language, which thy God
> Utters, who from eternity doth teach
> Himself in all, and all things in himself.
> Great universal Teacher! he shall mould
> Thy spirit, and by giving make it ask.

But the highest and final expression of the spirit of Unity and Necessity by Coleridge is to be found in the greatest poem of his life—*The Rime of the Ancient Mariner* (1797-8). This poem contains no reasoned religion, no obtrusive theological arguments, but merely the aroma, the fine flavor, the " breath and finer spirit " of the poet's religious meditations. And this almost against his will; for, as suggested in a note, he was consciously attempting to write a work of almost " pure imagination." His imagination, however, did not escape the shadow of all his previous religious musings, and the religious atmosphere of the poem is connected with the thought of all his earlier religious poems—is indeed its logical outcome.

Though dealing with other things besides religion, the poem is full of religious suggestiveness, whose source is not so much the supernatural machinery the poet uses, as that which is represented as taking place in the heart of the mariner. With all its charm, subtilty, unearthly music, and wild adventure, the poem indicates distinguishable stages in the mariner's moral and religious experience. Not the least marvel of the poem is the complete success with which Coleridge has rendered a spiritual experience by means of relating so wild a tale of strange adventure. Or, to put it otherwise, the wonder is that he has, without doing violence to either, fused such a tale and such an experience into an harmonious whole. If the poem ought to have had no more moral than an Arabian Night's tale, as Coleridge himself once suggested, it would have had to be completely rewritten and one of its most unique qualities destroyed.

The thing which makes this blending of religious experience and marvellous adventure possible, and successful, is chiefly the character of the mariner—one of the most distinctive creations in modern literature. Perhaps the most striking characteristic of the mariner is that in the story he does not act but is constantly acted upon—a fact which Wordsworth considered a great defect, but which for the purpose of the poem, is no defect at all. After the mariner had killed the albatross—an impulsive rather than a deliberative act—spirits and powers, plastic and vast, conjured up by the poet from the ends of the earth, played upon his mind and conscience as on a harp. Though in telling his own story the mariner has power over the will of the wedding-guest and over any who may be "predoomed" to listen to him, yet this power comes to him as a visitation and is not in his keeping. He has no will of his own; he is passive to the powers outside himself and the new law of life revealed to him; that is, he is a true Necessitarian:

> Forthwith this frame of mine was wrenched
> With a woful agony,
> Which forced me to begin my tale;
> And then it left me free.
>
> Since then, at an uncertain hour,
> That agony returns:
> And till my ghastly tale is told,
> This heart within me burns.
>
> I pass, like night, from land to land;
> I have strange power of speech;
> That moment that his face I see,
> I know the man that must hear me:
> To him my tale I teach.

In any other hands but those of Coleridge so passive a character would become insipid. But the mariner is saved from insipidity chiefly by the poet's communicating to him an unusual intensity of feeling. It is no doubt fitting that the ancient man should be " venerable, weather-beaten, and more or less oracular." It is also well that he has a glittering eye endowed with the power of fixing the attention of his listeners and of charming them, for a time, into that suspension of unbelief concerning the external events of the poem which constitutes poetic faith. But it is what goes on behind the glittering eye that really gives the eye its peculiar significance and power. It is what happens within the heart of the mariner that fixes him unforgettably in our imagination and makes him appeal to us humanly. Of the poem Charles Lamb wrote to Wordsworth: " I dislike all the miraculous parts of it, but the feeling of the man under the operation of such scenery, dragged me along like Tom Pipe's whistle. . . . The Ancient Mariner undergoes such trials as overwhelm and bury all individuality or memory of what he was— like the state of a man in a bad dream, one terrible peculiarity of which is, that all consciousness of personality is gone." The audacity of Coleridge's art in portraying the character, we may say, was to offset his passivity with such an intensity of feeling that he was on the verge of losing the sense of his own identity. This inward intensity, derived from Coleridge's own inwardness of mind, is the chief source of that exalted and sustained lyricism that gives unusual freshness and perpetual charm to the poem.

Simplicity and child-likeness of spirit further atone for the mariner's passivity. Though the character is old and weather-beaten, he throws himself with the absolute faith and complete *abandon* of a child into the telling of his story. This utter single-mindedness of the mariner bewitches the wedding-guest, and also the reader. Coleridge drank deep of the spirit of the folk ballad, and at no point has he more completely caught the primitive spirit of the ballads than in their child-likeness. It was a difficult feat for the poet to keep his own thought within the circle of the mariner's mind and the mariner's thought within the circle of a child's mind. At places where the mariner approaches generalizations and is in the greatest danger of becoming sophisticated, his thought and language become utterly simple and naïve. Such, for example, is the familiar passage near the end of the poem which, though hackneyed by constant quotation, expresses, with artistic grace, the sum of the mariner's religious wisdom. The poem, in short, is the most superb example of sustained naïveté in the language.

The failure to recognize the naïve spirit sufficiently has caused some critics who have taken seriously the moral of the poem to interpret certain important incidents erroneously. The killing, for example, of an albatross that persisted in following a ship for nine days would be considered according to eighteenth-century ethics trivial; and according to the scientific ethics of the twentieth century natural, or necessary, or, at any event, no great matter. But the mariner's ethics is that of a child. He killed the bird impulsively and wantonly. But when his fellow mariners attributed their fate and the fate of their ship, whether for good or evil, but chiefly for evil, to the killing of the albatross, and accounted the act a crime, he accepted without question their verdict; and straightway the crime became to him monstrous and overwhelming. He had no scale of values, and he suffered such intense agony as a child does when it is made to feel it has done an outrageously wicked thing, even though its compunction was of the slightest at the time of doing it. Perhaps no one has ever described more poignantly the prolonged agony that follows the inadvertent committal of a crime by an otherwise innocent person than has Coleridge, in the lines beginning with—

I looked to heaven, and tried to pray—

In truth, the sufferings and penances of the mariner are utterly out of proportion to the slightness of the crime. He is pursued by a dark and sinister fate. In his childlikeness he conceives the objects of nature as avenging personalities; the wind which drives the ship southward is the Storm Blast, tyrannous and strong, and the bloody and glorious Sun seems a living being, now appearing accusingly like a broad and burning face and now "like God's own head." The Moon and Stars and the Ocean are instinct with power and seem to conspire with the avenging Spirits against him. The only thing he can do is to lie passively under the terrifying strokes of fate and necessity. And because of the intensity of his feelings the mariner is the most effective, and because of his childlikeness he is the most attractive, Necessitarian in modern literature.

But the mariner is also a most engaging Unitarian. He

discourses sweetly and eloquently on the principle of universal love. To him, not good and evil, but love and loneliness are the two mighty contending forces in the Universe. In the story the mariner underwent an intense and suspended agony of spirit because of his separation, not merely from his comrades, but from the living world and from God:

> So lonely 'twas that God Himself
> Scarce seemed there to be.

To " abide alone " is more unendurable than flaming fire. But the mariner miraculously stood the test, although, as we have seen, he was all the while at the brink of losing consciousness of his own personality. At the same time he was intensely alive. The fate of his companions was a benediction as compared to the agony he endured in a living death. Those who hold that Coleridge violated poetic justice in the disposition he made of the crew either have a narrow conception of poetic justice or do not realize what it meant for the mariner to remain alive.

But love in the universe ultimately overcomes loneliness. The mariner had learned, not abstractly, but concretely, to love all things both great and small. And this wisdom of love, though childlike, had in Coleridge's day, and still has in ours, momentous implications. The eighteenth century had placed much emphasis on man's duty to man; it had taught that the proper study of mankind is man; it had sung the short and simple annals of the poor. But its teachings were based either on the principle of selfishness, which insisted that when you show kindness to your fellowmen you are advancing your own interests, or on the principle of benevolence, which was often quite coldhearted and full of mock pity. The new age, however, insisted on the Christian principle of becoming as little children in order to enter the kingdom of heaven. The note of it was struck in Blake's *Songs of Innocence,* its bearings worked out fully in the poems of Wordsworth, and its chief characteristics expressed in the person of the mariner by Coleridge. The new age also insisted that we have kinship, not merely with man, but with the whole animal creation. It may be urged that the instinctive affection a child shows for animals is based on an actual kinship with them, which is often ignored by adults, and was ignored especially by eighteenth-century philosophers. But this sense of kinship was asserted in the poetry of Cowper and of Burns; and in *The Ancient Mariner* Coleridge based it on the assumption that all creatures emanate from one Creator. This universal love gains its first victory in the poem when it is strong enough to make the mariner love the water-snakes. From that point it grows increasingly to the end, in larger and larger encircling reaches, till at last it embraces all living things in a sense of universal kinship, catching the mariner himself in its onward sweep, destining him in a necessitarian spirit to " pass, like night, from land to land " to tell the story of it, and causing him in particular to declare our universal human religious fellowship in one of the sweetest passages in our language, in the lines beginning with—

O sweeter than the marriage-feast—

Thus the spirit of *The Rime of the Ancient Mariner* is closely allied to the spirit of Coleridge's earlier religious poems. In *The Ancient Mariner* the poet, in his own inimitable manner, has given, in a rarefied etherealized form, the exhalations and aroma of his personal experience of Necessity and Unity, " the blossom and the fragrancy of all " his earlier religious meditations.[5]

[5] " Poetry is the blossom and the fragrancy of all human knowledge, human thought, human passions, emotions, language."—Coleridge, in *Biographia Literaria,* Chapter XV.

The Rime of the Ancient Mariner is also related to the earlier poems in the imagery it uses. In *The Destiny of Nations,* for example, the poet declares that since Fancy, by peopling the air with beings invisible, first unsensualizes the dark mind, he deems

> Those legends terrible, with which
> The polar ancient thrills his uncouth throng:
> Whether of pitying Spirits that make their moan
> O'er slaughter'd infants, or that giant bird
> Vuokho, of whose rushing wings the noise
> Is tempest, when the unutterable Shape
> Speeds from the mother of Death, and utters once
> That shriek, which never murderer heard, and lived.

Again, he says that in the far distant polar region

> Dwells the fury Form, whose unheard name,
> With eager eye, pale cheek, suspended breath
> And lips half-opening with the dread of sound
> Unsleeping Silence guards. . . . Yet the wizard her,
> Armed with Torngarsuck's power, the Spirit of Good,
> Forces to unchain the foodful progeny
> Of the Ocean's stream.[6]

"Wild phantasies!" Coleridge ejaculates. Wild and crude they are for the making of poetry. Yet these ancients, wizards, pitying Spirits, unutterable Shapes, and fury Forms of the polar regions suggest the direct origin of much of the imagery in *The Ancient Mariner,* where they become things of beauty. In the earlier poems these spirits and powers have an educative influence on character, " teaching reliance, and medicinal hope," and leading toward faith and truth; to which purpose they are put, in a far finer spirit, in *The Ancient Mariner*.

Imagery similar to this is to be found in the prose frag-

---

[6] The original sources of these passages are books of travel and history, such as Cranz's *History of Greenland*. The use Coleridge makes of them is all his own.

ment, *The Wanderings of Cain* (1798), as for instance: " There was no spring, no summer, no autumn; and the winter's snow, that would have been lovely, fell not on these hot rocks and scorching sands,"—which reminds one of the " hot and copper sky " of *The Ancient Mariner*.

The hero Cain, like the mariner, is a passive character, being pursued by mighty Powers: " The Mighty One that persecuteth me is on this side and on that; he pursueth my soul like the wind, like the sand-blast he passeth through me; he is around me even as the air! . . . The torrent that roareth far off hath a voice; and the clouds in heaven look terribly on me; the Mighty One who is against me speaketh in the wind of the cedar grove; and in silence am I dried up." There is never a saint to take pity on Cain's soul in agony: " The spirit within me is withered, and burnt up with extreme agony."

In the first part of *Christabel*, written in 1797, Coleridge came nearer realizing his ideal of producing a poem of " pure imagination " than in *The Rime of the Ancient Mariner*. Yet the heroine, the lovely Christabel, like the mariner, inadvertently lays herself open to a sinister influence. Again like the mariner and like Cain, she is a passive character and is pursued and wrought upon by an evil spirit. This evil being—a witch in the form of a beautiful and oppressed maiden who apparently flings herself upon the mercy of Christabel—is more hideous and terrifying to the imagination than anything else conceived by Coleridge. By enacting spells the witch usurps power over the maiden's utterances and works indescribable confusion in her heart.

If the earlier poems were too obtrusively religious, as compared to the subtile implications of *The Ancient Mariner,* the first part of *Christabel* has almost fallen out of religion on the other side. It is extremely fragile and verges on the shadowy and impalpable. In this direction, then, the evolution of Coleridge's mind has gone as far as possible.[7] Later Coleridge added a second part, which, however, does not come up to the first in the qualities just mentioned. And because of the extreme fragility of the first part Coleridge afterwards was never able to write up to its level and therefore never able to complete the poem, though for a time he consciously willed to do so. Yet in atmosphere as well as in general structure it is very similar to *The Ancient Mariner,* its first part closing with three lines that might have appeared in that poem:

> But this she knows, in joys and woes,
> That saints will aid if men will call:
> For the blue sky bends over all!

Had not Wordsworth suggested to Coleridge in *The Ancient Mariner* the incident of killing the albatross as a motive for punishing the mariner, it is doubtful whether Coleridge would have thought it necessary; for certainly in *Christabel,* a parallel case, the heroine has done nothing to merit the malignant persecution of the witch. In both cases Coleridge conceived that the sublime law of Necessitarian indifference would do its work effectively. For the verisimilitude to life in this principle he would have pointed to the manner in which his own footsteps had been dogged by an untoward fate.

Thus in this period Coleridge created none but passive, necessitarian-like characters, who are pursued by Shapes, Forms, Powers, Destinies, etc.; and wherever the story is completed the character is redeemed by universal love, and is reconciled to his world, the blue sky bending over all.

---

[7] It may be said that *Kubla Khan* (1798) advances a step farther. But from it have vanished logical structure and discoverable sequence of ideas; what remains is a fragment of pure esthetic luxury.

What was asserted rather crudely as religious opinion of Necessity and Unity in the early poems was swiftly transmuted into spiritual implications and expressed with subtile suggestiveness in the poems written in those few short years that constituted the flowering period of Coleridge's poetic genius.

II

TRANSCENDENTALISM

Late in his life Coleridge wrote concerning a poem of his youth, *The Destiny of Nations,* composed 1796: " Within twelve months after the writing of this Poem, my bold Optimism, and Necessitarianism, together with the Infra, seu plusquam-Socinianism, down to which, step by step, I had *un*believed, gave way to the day-break of a more genial and less shallow system. But I contemplate with pleasure these Phases of my Transition." Since Coleridge was often inaccurate concerning dates in his own life, it may be doubted whether this great change in his religious experience came as early as 1797 and as suddenly as he declares; for we have seen that the idea of Necessity continued to appear in his poems and writings after that time. The change seems to have come gradually and is not distinctly marked until around 1799, and later.

The first unmistakable sign of his change of heart is his attack upon the merely passive character of his former religious beliefs. In a letter to Thomas Poole, written early in 1801, he says: " Newton was a mere materialist. *Mind,* in his system, is always *passive,*—a lazy *Looker-on* on an external world. If the mind be not *passive,* if it be indeed made in God's Image, and that, too, in the sublimest sense, the *Image of the Creator,* there is ground for suspicion that any system built on the passiveness of the mind must be false as a system."[8] In another letter to Poole, written within a few days of the foregoing, he says: " If I do not greatly delude myself, I have not only *completely extricated the notion of time and space,* but have overthrown the doctrine of association, as taught by Hartley, and with it all the irreligious metaphysics of modern infidels—especially the doctrine of necessity." He thus repudiates not only an important phase of his earlier religious beliefs, but also his former teachers, on the basis of belief in the existence of a free, active energy in the mind of man; he is so far already committed to the transcendental principle.

Again, in 1803 he wrote concerning a certain necessitarian passage (written in 1794) as follows: " I utterly recant the sentiment contained in the lines—

[8] Against the Necessitarian, materialistic, and associational philosophies of the eighteenth century this charge of passiveness is made again and again in Coleridge's later writings—*The Friend, Biographia Literaria,* etc. It is striking that he should have made it so unequivocally thus early in this letter. He had remarkable prescience of truth which needed only the confirmation of other writers to bring it to maturity. One therefore can sympathize with his resentment against all attacks on him of plagiarism.

As if to make his renunciation irrevocable Coleridge a few years later (1804) again wrote to Poole: "I love and honour you, Poole, for many things; scarcely for anything more than that, trusting firmly in the rectitude and simplicity of your own heart, and listening with faith to its revealing voice, you never suffered either my subtlety, or my eloquence, to proselyte you to the pernicious doctrine of Necessity. All praise to the Great Being, who has graciously enabled me to find my way out of that labyrinth-den of sophistry, and I would fain believe, to bring with me a better clue than has hitherto been known to enable others to do the same." It might seem strange or absurd that a poet should feel an abasement of spirit for having held a certain metaphysical doctrine. But Coleridge was keenly aware that when he renounced this doctrine he was renouncing the whole trend and body of English thought from John Locke to William Godwin, and that a duty had been laid upon himself to find at least a working hypothesis to take its place.

> Of whose omniscient and all-spreading Love
> Aught to *implore* were impotence of mind,

it being written in Scripture, 'Ask, and it shall be given you,' and my human reason being moreover convinced of the propriety of offering *petitions* as well as thanksgiving to Deity." He thus accepted belief in Free-will; but only, it seems, after he had woven such strong threads of evil habits about his life that most of his career then seemed a sort of fatal necessity.

This new transcendental attitude of mind is indicated in a poem as early as 1799—*Lines Written in the Hartz Forest*. The theme of the poem is expressed in the lines—

> For I had found
> That outward forms, the loftiest, still receive
> Their finer influence from the Life within;—
> Fair cyphers else; fair, but of import vague
> Or unconcerning.

He illustrates this by saying that though standing on the height of the Brocken in Germany his eye shaped before him in the steady clouds the sands and high white cliffs of England (which he loved) so vividly that all the view

> From sovran Brocken, woods and woody hills,
> Floated away, like a departing dream,
> Feeble and dim!

Thus outward forms depend, for their beauty, upon what the perceiving mind contributes to them; mind is the active agency in determining the nature and quality of perception. The poet asserts that this matter must not be taken lightly, although he humbly admits that that man shows a sublimer spirit who can feel

> That God is everywhere! the God who framed
> Mankind to be one mighty family,
> Himself our Father, and the World our Home.

Not a little interest may be attached to the fact that this poem, which for the first time in Coleridge's poetry expresses the transcendental conception of the might of the mind, should have been written in Germany, whither the poet had gone to study German philosophy. Yet it is practically certain that at this time he had but the slightest knowledge of Kant. Still, a meager knowledge only of that author together with the growth of his own many-sided interests would be sufficient to account for his having arrived at the sense of the shallowness of his former conceptions, especially as regards Necessity, or the passiveness of the mind.

And now, having outgrown the superficialities of his eighteenth-century teachers, Coleridge, at about the age of thirty, mature and unusually endowed and equipped, stood at the threshold of a period in which we should expect him to become the great transcendental and religious poet of his age. But in this we are almost completely disappointed. There are only a few straggling poems as a record of his achievement. His prose, upon which he spent his greatest efforts, is also fragmentary.

Various reasons have been assigned for Coleridge's failure in poetry. Some of them are obvious, others more subtile. Rheumatism and other physical ailments, and the use of opium, which became a confirmed habit with him about 1801, go far in explaining the failure. Subtler and even more potent causes were a congenital weakness of will and the lack of any sure anchorage in home affections.

Perhaps a more serious cause was a strong natural tendency in Coleridge toward the abstract. Stopford Brooke says that Coleridge had the power, in a far greater degree than other poets, of "impassionating himself about intellectual conceptions." This is true of Coleridge up to about 1799, but not thereafter. Indeed, he later more than once expressed a yearning for just this power, which had now left him. Two essential and indispensable feelings had departed—joy and hope. Without these he could not impassionate himself even about intellectual conceptions. For

> Work without Hope draws nectar in a sieve,
> And Hope without an object cannot live.
> *(Work Without Hope*, 1827)

We have already seen that there was a tendency to abstractions in Coleridge's earliest poetry, but that a little later he succeeded in rendering these in his best poetry in terms of concrete representation, imaginative suggestion, and deep feeling. But now, bereft of some essential feelings, he swung more strongly than ever toward abstractions. It was not that at a certain time in his life he began the study of German metaphysics which destroyed the poet in him, as so many critics declare — his own new position, "we receive but what we give," refutes the critics—it was simply that in the long run his original natural impulse to abstractions was stronger in him than the impulse to concrete poetical representation. Coleridge's prime interest in life was religion; but a man who would be the poet of a transcendental religion must look well to the simple, emotional, and picturing side of his art. The great central antinomy which lies at the root of Coleridge's prose—the superiority of Reason over mere Understanding—he was not able to render successfully into story, incident, and poetic imaginings.

Moreover, as regards poetic method, Coleridge had perfected his art between the years 1794 and 1799. We saw how in that period his imagination made use of witches, wizards, polar spirits, etc., in a crude way in the earlier poems, but in a way nothing short of marvellous in *The Ancient Mariner* and *Christabel*. This imagery was perfectly adapted to that kind of poetry. Coleridge's use of it had become a habit, which was not easily to be shaken off. But this method of poetic representation was in no wise suited to a serious religious poetry that was to exalt the free powers of the mind and soul of man. It was almost literally necessary that he begin again at the beginning to develop an appropriate poetical method. No wonder that his "shaping spirit of Imagination" could not adapt itself to his new material and his new way of thinking! [9]

Most of these failings are attested by Coleridge himself in the poem *Dejection: An Ode,* written in 1802. This poem also gives the fullest expression to be found in his poetry of the transcendental principle. Around the statement of this principle, set in the center of the poem, the poet weaves his personal experiences, which, in turn, are set against an external background of evening and night, gradually shifting from an ominous calm to a raging storm.

The poet is possessed with a feeling of dull pain; the western sky, clouds, stars, and the moon can make no impression on his failing spirits:

> I see them all so excellently fair,
> I see, not feel, how beautiful they are!

His capacity for thinking remains unimpaired; but the sources of his feelings are dried up,—he cannot get relief from external Nature:

---

[9] Those who suppose that if his poetical powers had remained unimpaired Coleridge would have continued writing *Ancient Mariners* and *Christabels* imagine a vain thing. He never had an exalted opinion of *The Ancient Mariner* and did not publish *Christabel* until urged by Byron. In fact, these poems did not represent for him the highest truth of life after 1799.

> I may not hope from outward forms to win
> The passion and the life, whose fountains are within.

Therefore it naturally follows that

> O Lady! we receive but what we give,
> And in our life alone does Nature live; . . .
> Ah! from the soul itself must issue forth
> A light, a glory, a fair luminous cloud
>   Enveloping the Earth—
> And from the soul itself must there be sent
>   A sweet and potent voice, of its own birth,
> Of all sweet sounds the life and element!

This generalization, which may be said to be the theme of the poem, is as radical transcendentalism as some of the poet's earlier conceptions were radical necessitarianism. The mind now is not an automaton, but an original creative force; nature becomes a mirror, a mere mechanical instrument, in which man's mind can reflect itself. All the color, warmth, beauty, life, and life's effluence, which we usually ascribe to outer Nature, are really derived from some inward energy of the soul.

Now this energizing force, this inward light, "this beautiful and beauty-making power" of the soul, the poet goes on to say, is Joy:

> Joy, Lady! is the spirit and the power,
> Which wedding Nature to us gives in dower
>   A new Earth and new Heaven,
> Undreamt of by the sensual and the proud—
> Joy is the sweet voice, Joy the luminous cloud—
>   We in ourselves rejoice!
> And thence flows all that charms or ear or sight,
>   All melodies the echoes of that voice,
> All colours a suffusion from that light.

There was a time when the poet's joy dallied with distress, yet hope still remained with him. Now, however, both joy and hope have fled:

> But now afflictions bow me down to earth:
> Nor care I that they rob me of my mirth;
> But oh! each visitation
> Suspends what nature gave me at my birth,
> My shaping spirit of Imagination.

Abstruse research, he says, became his sole resource, his only plan,

> Till that which suits a part infects the whole,
> And now is almost grown the habit of my soul.

The poet is aroused from his revery by the ravings of the night-wind, which symbolizes his own mental unrest and peoples his mind with wild phantasies of a mad host in rout and of a little child lost in a storm. He concludes by pronouncing upon the Lady of the poem that benediction of joy which he himself does not possess. But here we must quote the poem as it originally appeared, which was addressed throughout, not to a Lady, but to the poet Wordsworth:

> O rais'd from anxious dread and busy care,
> By the immenseness of the good and fair
> Which thou see'st everywhere,
> Joy lifts thy spirit, joy attunes thy voice,
> To thee do all things live from pole to pole,
> Their life the eddying of thy living soul!
> O simple spirit, guided from above,
> O lofty Poet, full of life and love,
> Brother and friend of my devoutest choice,
> Thus may'st thou ever, evermore rejoice!

The importance of this poem in Coleridge's spiritual history cannot easily be overestimated. The poet may be taken at his word, although literalness must not be carried too far. For instance, it is not to be concluded that Coleridge did not live many pleasant days after he had written this poem. Nevertheless it is strictly true that the kind of joy necessary for the working of his creative imagination never returned to him. Abstruse research, abstract reasonings, were the only substitutes possible. Had he had a profound conviction, such as Poe's, that sorrow and melancholy are the best themes for poetry, he undoubtedly could have written many marvellous poems in a doleful spirit. But like Wordsworth he held that truly creative art must be inspired by joy, that poetry is the spontaneous overflow of powerful emotions. The poet, Coleridge held, must be full of life and love, must have a sense of the immenseness of the good and fair; he must "bring the whole soul of man into activity, with the subordination of its faculties to each other according to their relative worth and dignity"[10]— imagination, will, intellect, emotion; not only must he have fine perceptions of spiritual truth, but his soul must be able, by an inward active energy, to create even the life and the element of what it perceives. The contrast between this high transcendental and spiritual conception as an ideal of his art and the utterly depressing mood and waning power of the poet himself, at the age of thirty, is as pathetic as anything in literary history. With a grace equal to its pathos he deferred to one who he deemed had the requisite qualifications—Wordsworth.

Seldom thereafter did he allow himself to sing in a strain similar to this — once in the poem *To William Wordsworth,* written in 1807, after he had read Wordsworth's *Prelude.* Here he asserts again the transcendental principle of the self-determining power of the mind, "the dread watch-tower of man's absolute self," as he describes Wordsworth's singing of

> Currents self-determined, as might seem,
> Or by some inner Power; of moments awful,

---

[10] *Biographia Literaria.* See the whole passage, close of chapter XIV.

> Now in thy inner life, and now abroad,
> When power streamed from thee, and thy soul received
> The light reflected, as the light bestowed.

In sharp contrast to this conception is Coleridge's own mood of

> Fears self-willed, that shunned the eye of hope;
> And hope that scarce would know itself from fear;
> Sense of past youth, and manhood come in vain,
> And genius given, and knowledge won in vain.

These passages are strikingly similar to the corresponding passages in *Dejection: An Ode;* [11] only, the disparity between the poet's ideal and his prevailing mood is even greater here than in the earlier poem. He recognizes with bitterness the impossibility of ever realizing his ideal in poetry. Yet he consoles himself with the thought that

> Peace is nigh
> Where wisdom's voice has found a listening heart.

But in poetry the world demands a producer, not a listener. However, if Coleridge could not produce the poetry his heart could pronounce good, he would remain silent; and silent he remained as a poet almost literally the rest of his life.

Hymn Before Sunrise, in the Vale of Chamouni [12] (1802), five years earlier than *To William Wordsworth* and about the same time as *Dejection: An Ode,* aims to be more specifically religious than the other two poems, and shows a strong tendency toward the abstract:

---

[11] The passages beginning respectively with, "O Lady! we receive but what we give," and, "But now afflictions bow me down to earth."

[12] For his conception Coleridge was indebted to the poem *Chamouni at Sun-rise*, by Frederike Brun, a German poetess. But Coleridge, as DeQuincey said, "created the dry bones of the German outlines into fulness of life."

> O dread and silent Mount! I gazed upon thee,
> Till thou, still present to the bodily sense,
> Didst vanish from my thought: entranced in prayer
> I worshipped the Invisible alone.

The poet's Thought, or Reason, comes into perfect union with God,

> Till the dilating Soul, enrapt, transfused,
> Into the mighty vision passing—there
> As in her natural form, swelled vast to Heaven!

In *Dejection: An Ode* Coleridge conceives the finer aspects of Nature as possessing what the mind of man contributes to them; in *Hymn Before Sunrise* he asserts a complementary truth, namely, that Nature herself is but a tool, a mouth-piece, of the Mind of the Divine. The stupendous mountain, the wild torrents thundering down the " precipitous, black, jagged rocks," the vale beneath, all gorgeously described, are but so many voices attesting the omnipotence of God:

> Thou kingly Spirit throned among the hills,
> Thou dread ambassador from Earth to Heaven,
> Great Hierarch! tell thou the silent sky,
> And tell the stars, and tell yon rising sun
> Earth, with her thousand voices, praises God.

The Mind of God and the Reason of Man are the two sovereign entities of existence; the objects of Nature are but the reflex of either:

> Whene'er the mist, that stands 'twixt God and thee,
> Defecates to a pure transparency,
> That intercepts no light and adds no stain—
> There Reason is, and then begins her reign! [13]

Hymn Before Sunrise is full of exclamatory sentences, suggesting that the poet had difficulty in lifting his emo-

---

[13] But he also quotes Dante to the effect that such Reason is unattainable.

tions and style to the height of his great argument. And unless interfused by correspondingly deep emotions its profound abstract conception yields more fruit for prose than for poetry.

Both the expressed and the suggested transcendental ideas in the poems we have just been considering are fully drawn out in *The Friend,* a series of essays published as a weekly periodical in 1809 and 1810, and revised and published in book form in 1818. The display of immense learning and wide reading, the unusually large number of latinized words and complicated sentences, the extraordinary subtile and abstract reasonings, show that Coleridge gave free rein to that intellectual and abstracting power of the mind for which he was famed among his contemporaries.

By 1809 Coleridge was deeply immersed in the study of German metaphysics, which confirmed and helped to develop his own transcendental philosophy. Though for a time Schelling was in the ascendency, Kant in the long run was the most important influence. The works of Kant, Coleridge frankly asserts in *Biographia Literaria,* "took possession of me as with the giant's hand." Kant gave him the conviction of the essential difference between Reason and Understanding—a fundamental position in *The Friend.* But Coleridge was no mere imitator of Kant. For his great principle of method he was indebted to Plato and Bacon as well as to Kant. To Coleridge, whose reasonings, though subtile, were never rigidly logical, Plato's 'Ideas,' Bacon's 'Laws,' and Kant's 'Intuitive Reason' were all very much the same.[14] And with them he interwove something distinctly his own.[15]

---

[14] "That which, contemplated objectively (that is, as existing externally to the mind), we call a law; the same contemplated subjectively (that is, as existing in a subject or mind), is an idea.

Though *The Friend* was too cumbrous to achieve with the reading public either an immediate or an ultimate success, its general drift is at once clear and positive. Its aim, vigorously stated by the author in parts of two sentences, is " to support all old and venerable truths; and by them to support, to kindle, to protect the spirit; to make the reason spread light over our feelings, to make our feelings, with their vital warmth, actualize our reason; "—" to refer men's opinions to their absolute principles,[16] and thence their feelings to the appropriate objects and in their due degrees; and finally, to apply the principles thus ascertained to the formation of steadfast convictions concerning the most important questions of politics, morality, and religion." The venerable truths of the Bible, of the Ancient Classics, and of Elizabethan and Puritan poets and statesmen and divines [17] are mar-

Hence Plato often names ideas laws; and Lord Bacon, the British Plato, describes the laws of the material universe as the ideas in nature."—Coleridge in *Constitution of Church and State*.

[15] In addition to the reason already given why it is almost impossible to track Coleridge in his borrowings from numberless authors, is his conception of the nature of truth. First: " I regard truth as a divine ventriloquist: I care not from whose mouth the sounds are supposed to proceed, if only the words are audible and intelligible." Secondly, he conceived truth as a process and a growth, and his own intellect as in a state of development, and therefore changing. Those who try to specify narrowly his indebtedness are inevitably driven to use such words as ' probably,' ' perhaps,' ' reasonable to suppose,' etc.

[16] The words ' refer,' ' ground,' ' bottom,' ' deduce,' used in the sense of grounding or bottoming opinions in principles, or of deducing them from principles, are great favorites with Coleridge.

[17] " Conscious that in upholding some priciples both of taste and philosophy, adopted by the great men of Europe, from the middle of the fifteenth till toward the close of the seventeenth century, I must run counter to many prejudices of many of my readers,— " Wordsworth is the only contemporary quoted approvingly, and in the 1818 edition he is quoted oftener than any other single writer.

shalled to do service in the cause of a transcendental religion.

The absolute principle in man, which gives him ultimate assurance of his higher spiritual and religious nature, in whch his experiences must be grounded, and to which all his opinions must be referred, is Reason:

> Reason! best and holiest gift of God and bond of union with the giver;—the high title by which the majesty of man claims precedence above all other living creatures;—mysterious faculty, the mother of conscience, of language, of tears, and of smiles;—calm and incorruptible legislator of the soul, without whom all its other powers would "meet in oppugnancy";—sole principle of permanence amid endless change,—in a world of discordant appetites and imagined self-interests the only common measure. . . . Thou alone, more than even the sunshine, more than the common air, art given to all men, and to every man alike (Section I, Essay II).

Reason is absolute, and therefore "is the same in all men, is not susceptible of degree:" it is impersonal, making men "feel within themselves a something ineffably greater than their own individual nature;" it is the organ of the supersensuous and of an inward sense, therefore it has "the power of acquainting itself with invisible realities or spiritual objects"; it implies free-will and conscience, giving "to every rational being the right of acting as a free agent, and of finally determining his conduct by his own will, according to his own conscience." "Man must be free; or to what purpose was he made a spirit of reason, and not a machine of instinct? Man must obey; or wherefore has he a conscience? The powers, which create this difficulty, contain its solution likewise: for their service is perfect freedom."

A faculty in man lower than reason and sharply distinguished from it is the understanding,—the instrument, so to speak, of reason. For "reason never acts by itself, but must clothe itself in the substance of individual understanding and specific inclination, in order to become a reality and an object of consciousness and experience." The understanding is not absolute but relative, " possessed in very different degrees by different persons," according to their enlightenment by past experience and immediate observation; it is not impersonal but personal, " the whole purport and functions of which consist in individualization, in outlines and differencings by quantity and relation"; it is not an organ of the supersensuous, but " a faculty of thinking and forming judgments on the notices furnished by sense," selecting, organizing, and generalizing; it does not imply free-will, but acts within the laws of cause and effect with reference to prudence and practical expediency.

Lower than the understanding in man are the organs of sense: "Under the term 'sense' I comprise," says Coleridge, " whatever is passive in our being, without any reference to the question of materialism or immaterialism; all that man is in common with animals, in kind at least— his sensations, and impressions " [18] (Section I, Essay III).

From these principles as a working basis Coleridge attempts to interpret the ultimate realities of politics, morality, and religion. As to politics, government is a science of relativity, which concerns itself with the owner-

[18] " When I make a threefold distinction in human nature, I am fully aware, that it is a distinction, not a division, and that in every act of mind the man unites the properties of sense, understanding, and reason. Nevertheless it is of great practical importance, that these distinctions should be made and understood. . . . They are more than once expressed, and everywhere supposed, in the writings of St. Paul. I have no hesitation in undertaking to prove, that every heresy which has disquieted the Christian Church, from Tritheism to Socinianism, has originated in and supported itself by arguments rendered plausible only by the confusion of these faculties, and thus demanding for the objects of one, a sort of evidence appropriated to those of another faculty " (Section I, Essay III).

ship and distribution of property, and with the physical well-being and the security of the individuals who make up a nation. To gain these ends " we must rely upon our understandings, enlightened by past experiences and immediate observation, and determining our choice by comparisons of expediency," giving heed to " particular circumstances, which will vary in every different nation, and in the same nation at different times." That is, the understanding, rather than reason, must be the chief active faculty to determine the affairs of government. It follows, on the one hand, that man is not to be governed by fear, or the power of the stronger, as though he were a mere creature of the senses; and, on the other, that man cannot, in the political aspect, be governed by 'pure reason,' which is absolute, impersonal, and transcendental. The system of Hobbes is an example of the former, which Coleridge dismisses with contempt as a system that " applies only to beasts." [19] An example of the latter is Rousseau's *Social Contract,* which mistakenly exalts matters of the understanding, relative, personal, prudential, into the realm of pure reason, thus giving unlimited range to a wild and dangerous individualism. Reason, grounded in morality and conscience, is not possessed by men collectively, but by individuals.[20] It is a wise govern-

---

[19] Hobbes's system " denies all truth and distinct meaning of the words, right and duty; and affirming that the human mind consists of nothing but the manifold modifications of passive sensations, considers men as the highest sort of animals indeed, but at the same time the most wretched."—This is one of the many severe strictures of Coleridge on all systems in which " at all events the minds of men were to be sensualized " and reduced to a passive state.

[20] Coleridge does ample justice to Rousseau's disquisitions on pure reason and free-will as inalienable qualities in man's being. But these high powers must not be abased to the use of expediency and worldly prudence which are primarily requisite in matters of gov-

ment that recognizes the inviolability of this reason in individuals and makes no regulations to interfere with its freedom. It will content itself " to regulate the outward actions of particular bodies of men, according to their particular circumstances," being guided largely by the enlightened intelligence of its public men. Thus reason acts as a constant corrective on the various phases of governmental changes and growth; so that

> The dignity of human nature will be secured, and at the same time a lesson of humility taught to each individual, when we are made to see that the universal necessary laws, and pure ideas of reason, were given us not for the purpose of flattering our pride, and enabling us to become national legislators; but that, by an energy of continued self-conquest we might establish a free and yet absolute government in our own spirits (Section I, Essay III).[21]

It is, then, by the cultivation of individual morality and religion rather than by politics that the impersonal and absolute reason residing in the breast of every human being may incorporate itself in a thousand forms in all the inclinations and activities of the personal and relative understandings of men, and through their understandings subdue and regulate the life of their senses, thus devel-

---

ernment. Therefore Rousseau's system, he argues, " as an exclusive total, is under any form impracticable."

[21] The changes in Coleridge's political views correspond to the changes in his religious development. In 1795, when he was in strong sympathy with the French Revolution, he recommended, in his Bristol address, " a practical faith in the doctrine of philosophical Necessity " as a panacea for the troubled times. In 1798, when he had lost faith in the leadership of France for liberty, he expressed the doubt, in *France: An Ode*, whether liberty could make its home anywhere but in the realm of Nature—" nor ever didst breathe thy soul in forms of human power." In 1809 he expressed the idea that true liberty is to be wrought out, not by means of political legislation, but in the souls of men in a transcendental spirit of self-conquest. Political government is thus the outcome, not the cause, of liberty.

oping men to their highest capacities and making them free indeed.

Morality and religion are essentially one. They "cannot be disjoined without the destruction of both." Whenever they are partially disjoined it invariably follows that a short-sighted scheme of prudence, based on the mere evidence of "sensible concretes," the rule of expediency, "which properly belongs to one and the lower part of morality," will be made the whole. To substitute this worldly prudence "for the laws of reason and conscience," Coleridge says, "or even to confound them under one name, is a prejudice, say rather a profanation, which I became more and more reluctant to flatter by even an appearance of assent." Reason, therefore, the organ of the supersensuous and transcendental, with all that it implies of conscience, free-will, and faith,[22] is the sole arbiter of the inseparable forces of our moral and religious experience.

Philosophy, understood and pursued in the right spirit, is an important aid to religion. The aim of philosophy is to discover the absolute principles of existence, to find for all that exists conditionally "a ground that is unconditional and absolute, and thereby to reduce the aggregate of human knowledge to a system." But to reason at all on principles of the absolute the mind must have some kind of power to go out of its individual, personal self, and must think and act in accord with some discoverable method. By his emphasis on the science of method and on mental initiative as a prerequisite to all experiments

[22] "What is faith, but the personal realization of the reason by its union with the will?" (Section II, Essay II). "Faith is a total act of the soul: it is the whole state of the mind, or it is not at all; and in this consists its power, as well as its exclusive worth" (Section I, Essay xv).

and investigations Coleridge felt he had made his most distinctive contribution to religious philosophy.

This principle of method is operative in our hourly and daily experiences, is the condition of our intellectual progress, and may " be said even to constitute the science of education, alike in the narrowest and in the most extensive sense of the word." The educated man is superior to the uneducated in this, that by a previous act and conception of the mind he selects with method the relative from the irrelative, the significant from the insignificant. Dame Quickly's want of method, old Polonius's form of method without its substance, and Hamlet's superb method when he is at his best, are examples of Shakespeare's mastery of this fundamental " principle of progressive transition." In short, all the failures in education may be ascribed to the " inattention to the method dictated by nature herself, to the simple truth, that as the forms in all organized existence, so much all true and living knowledge proceeds from within."

In scientific and speculative thought the prime materials of method are the relations of objects, and the contemplation of relations is the indispensable condition of thinking methodically. There are two kinds of relations —that of law and that of theory. The first is of " the absolute kind which, comprehending in itself the substance of every possible degree, precludes from its conception all degree, not by generalization, but by its own plenitude "; it is an attribute of the Supreme Being, inseparable from the idea of God, and from it must be derived all true insight into all other grounds and principles necessary to method. The second is a process of generalization and supposes the ideas of cause and effect, being illustrated in the scientific arts of medicine, chemistry, and physiology. Between the first (law as absolute) and the second (theory as relative) lies the method in the fine arts, which outwardly are governed by the position of parts and mechanical relations, etc., while inwardly they contain that which originates in the artist himself and which partakes of the absolute. Thus it is implied that the first relation is of higher value than the second, that the results obtainable by the second are at best but approximations of the first.

In philosophy Plato most perfectly illustrated the principles of mental initiative and of method. The larger and more valuable of Plato's works have one common end—" to establish the sources, to evolve the principles, and exemplify the art of method. . . . The education of the intellect, by awakening the principle and method of self-development was his proposed object, not any specific information that can be conveyed into it from without." But this mental initiative, which is reason itself, has its ultimate source in a supersensual essence, the pre-establisher of the harmony between the laws of matter and the ideas of pure intellect. Thus for Plato philosophy ends in religion.

By showing that these same principles of method and of intellectual intuition—*lumen siccum*—were fundamental in Bacon's philosophic works Coleridge effected the so-called reconciliation of Plato and Bacon. Their very differences—that Plato sought the truth by applying the principle of method to the intellect, and that Bacon sought it by applying the principle of method to nature—tends only to accentuate the fact that their principles at bottom are one and the same.

Indeed the reconcilement of Plato and Bacon is but one instance of the larger use Coleridge aims to make of the principle of method. He employs it as the means of reconciling all opposites. " Extremes meet " is to him a divine aphorism. " All method supposes a principle of unity with progression; in other words, progressive transition without breach of continuity." Even in the world of the senses an organism exists only by virtue of possessing " corresponding opposites " held in unity, and derives its character from an antecedent method of self-organizing purpose, the impulse of which comes from something above nature and is transcendental.[23] Likewise man's understanding grows by a similar process of reconciling " opposite yet interdependent forces," whose organizing impulse is derived from pure reason. The similarity of the processes in nature and in the understanding makes it possible for the understanding to comprehend nature; thus by constant self-effort in experimenting and generalizing the understanding is led to comprehend gradually and progressively the relation of each to the other, of each to all—to perceive the world in unity and arrive at a general affirmation of the reality of a supreme being.

But here the understanding (the dialectic intellect) stops. Says Coleridge:

It is utterly incapable of communicating insight or conviction concerning the existence or possibility of the world, as different from Deity. It finds itself constrained to identify, more truly to confound, the Creator with the aggregate of his creature. . . . The inevitable result of all consequent reasoning, in which the intellect refuses to acknowledge a higher or deeper ground than it can itself supply, and weens to possess within itself the centre of its own system, is—and from Zeno the Eleatic to Spinoza, and from Spinoza to the Schellings, Okens and their adherents, of the present day, ever has been—pantheism under one or other of its modes, the least

---

[23] Man derives his sense of reality of the objects of nature from an experience which " compels him to contemplate as without and independent of himself what yet he could not contemplate at all, were it not a modification of his own being " (Section II, Essay XI). This re-emphasizes that " in our life alone does nature live," as asserted in *Dejection: An Ode* (1802).

repulsive of which differs from the rest, not in its consequences, which are one and the same in all, and in all alike are practically atheistic, but only as it may express the striving of the philosopher himself to hide these consequences from his own mind. This, therefore, I repeat, is the final conclusion. All speculative disquisition must begin with postulates, which the conscience alone can at once authorize and substantiate: and from whichever point the reason may start, from the things which are seen to the one invisible, or from the idea of the absolute one to the things that are seen, it will find a chasm, which the moral being only, which the spirit and religion of man alone, can fill up.

Thus I prefaced my inquiry into the science of method with a principle deeper than science, more certain than demonstration. . . . There is but one principle, which alone reconciles the man with himself, with others, and with the world; which regulates all relations, tempers all passions, gives power to overcome or support all suffering, and which is not to be shaken by aught earthly, for it belongs not to the earth: namely, the principle of religion, the living and substantial faith *which passeth all understanding*, as the cloud-piercing rock, which overhangs the stronghold of which it had been the quarry and remains the foundation; . . . this it is which affords the sole sure anchorage in the storm, and at the same time the substantiating principle of all true wisdom, the satisfactory solution of all the contradictions of human nature, of the whole riddle of the world (Section II, Essay xi).

This remarkable passage and the following, which emphasizes the soul's freedom and immortality, reveal the heart of Coleridge's spiritual consciousness and the central springs of the philosophy of *The Friend:*

God created man in his own image. To be the image of his own eternity created he man! Of eternity and self-existence what other likeness is possible, but immortality and moral self-determination? In addition to sensation, perception, and practical judgment—instinctive or acquirable—concerning the notices furnished by the organs of perception, all which in kind at least, the dog possesses in common with his master; in addition to these, God gave us reason, and with reason he gave us reflective self-consciousness; gave us principles, distinguished from the maxims and generalisations of outward experience by their absolute and essential universality and necessity, and above all, by superadding to reason the mysterious faculty of free-will and consequent personal amenability, he gave us conscience—that law of conscience, which in the power, and as the indwelling word, of a holy and omnipotent legislator . . . unconditionally commands us to attribute reality, and actual existence, to those ideas and to those only, without which the conscience itself would be baseless and contradictory, to the ideas of soul, of free-will, of immortality, and of God. To God, as the reality of the conscience and the source of all obligation; to free-will, as the power of the human being to maintain the obedience which God through the conscience has commanded, against all the might of nature; and to the immortality of the soul, as a state in which the weal and woe of man shall be proportioned to his moral worth. With this faith all nature,

—all the mighty world
of eye and ear—

presents itself to us, now as the aggregated material of duty, and now as a vision of the Most High revealing to us the mode, and time, and particular instance of applying and realizing that universal rule, pre-established in the heart of our reason (Introduction, Essay xv).

The Hebrew Scriptures alone give an adequate account of these high matters. The Greeks made brilliant discoveries in the region of pure intellect and are still unrivalled in the arts of the imagination. The Romans were given " to war, empire, law." " It was the Roman instinct to appropriate by conquest and give fixure by legislation." But

The Hebrews may be regarded as the fixed mid point of the living line, toward which the Greeks as the ideal pole, and the Romans as the material, were ever approximating; till the coincidence and final synthesis took place in Christianity, of which the Bible is the law, and Christendom the *phenomenon* (Section II, Essay x).

The prose treatise *Aids to Reflection* (1825) has the same general atmosphere and outlook as *The Friend;* it employs again the principles of method and mental initiative and the distinction between reason and understanding as bases for interpreting morality and religion; and it asserts with equal emphasis that religion is the ultimate reality of life.

On the other hand, *Aids to Reflection* is much less subtile and abstruse, has a clearer outline and a more orderly arrangement of its matter, and is altogether a more readable book. Its frankly aphoristic style saves its author from the pitfalls of over-ingenuity which abound in *The Friend*. Not as arbitrary in its logic, it becomes a more profoundly human document. It admits of more latitude in argument and of greater flexibility in its distinctions. Reason, which in *The Friend* had been considered purely an absolute principle, is divided into speculative and practical reason, the speculative dealing with formal or abstract truth, the practical with actual, or moral, truth. Prudence, thought of in *The Friend* as at best a very low form of morality that stands in opposition to higher spiritual life, is more reasonably admitted into the scheme of true morality. Though *The Friend* asserted that the reason recognizes the will and conscience as important agencies in man's spiritual development, *Aids to Reflection* exalts the will relatively to a more prominent position. Though the former work recognized Christianity as the true religion, the latter lifts it to a place of central interest in the reader's consciousness; what was implicit concerning Christianity in the former becomes explicit in the latter, in accordance with the natural evolution of Coleridge's mind.

In short, Coleridge's main purpose in *Aids to Reflection* is to harmonize the tenets and doctrines of orthodox Christianity with his own transcendental philosophy; to " translate the terms of theology into their moral equivalents "; as, for example, to render such words as " sanctifying influences of the Spirit " by " purity in life and action from a pure principle," or to contemplate the words " spirit, grace, gifts, operations, and the like " as ideas of " the reason, flowing naturally from the admission of an infinite omnipresent mind as the ground of the universe," with the aim of giving a fresh and deeper meaning to the old truths of religion. The inspiration and high hope of his work was that he might, in humility and modesty, "form the human mind anew after the Divine Image."

"The requisites," he says, "for the execution of this high intent may be comprised under three heads: the prudential, the moral, and the spiritual. . . . The prudential corresponds to the sense and the understanding; the moral to the heart and the conscience; the spiritual to the will and the reason, that is, to the finite will reduced to harmony with, and in subordination to, the reason, as a ray from the true light which is both reason and will, universal reason, and will absolute." This threefold classification is logically adhered to in the three main divisions of the book, under the heads respectively of Prudential Aphorisms, Moral and Religious Aphorisms, and Aphorisms of Spiritual Religion Indeed.

Moral prudence is mainly prohibitive; *Thou shalt not* is its most characteristic formula. Its danger is to develop mere self-protection and self-love, and it must never be substituted for, or confused with, the higher morality. As a corrective on our sensual nature and as a protector of virtue it is a necessity; it acts as a sort of doorway between the world of the senses and morality. "Though prudence in itself is neither virtue nor spiritual holiness, yet without prudence, or in opposition to it, neither virtue nor holiness can exist."

Higher than prudence is religious morality. Here are opened up at once questions concerning the relation of some of the essential doctrines of Christianity to the feelings, motives, the conscience, and the will, of man. Christianity, for instance, is superior to Stoicism in this, that while the latter attaches honor to the person who acts virtuously in spite of his feelings, the former "instructs us to place small reliance on a virtue that does not begin by bringing the feelings to a conformity with the commands of the conscience. Its especial aim, its characteristic operation, is to moralize the feelings."

Again, such phrases from the Scriptures as *the Spirit beareth witness with our spirit* cannot be explained except by postulating the freedom of the will in man: "The man makes the motive, and not the motive the man. What is a strong motive to one man, is no motive at all to another. If, then, the man determines the motive, what determines the man—to a good and worthy act, we will say, or a virtuous course of conduct? The intelligent will, or the self-determined power? True, in part it is: and therefore the will is pre-eminently, the spiritual constituent in our being." It is only with a free, spiritual being that we can imagine the Spirit to hold intercommunion.

Being spiritual, the will is not natural, that is, not in nature:

Whatever is comprised in the chain and mechanism of cause and effect, of course necessitated, and having its necessity in some other thing, antecedent or concurrent—this is said to be natural; and the aggregate and system of all such things is Nature. It is, therefore, a contradiction in terms to include in this the free-will, of which the verbal definition is—that which originates an act or state of being. . . . . It follows, therefore, that whatever originates its own acts, or in any sense contains in itself the cause of its own state, must be spiritual, and consequently supernatural; yet not on that account necessarily miraculous. And such must the responsible Will in us be, if it be at all. . . . These views of the Spirit, and of the Will as spiritual, form the ground-work of my scheme.[24]

(*On Spiritual Religion Indeed*, Introduction to Aphorism x)

---

[24] "I have attempted, then, to fix the proper meaning of the words, Nature and Spirit, the one being the *antithesis* to the other: so that the most general and negative definition of nature is, whatever is

This conception of the will as above Nature and above the law of cause and effect is in flat contradiction to the philosophy of the Necessitarians, who assume " that motives act on the will, as bodies act on bodies; and that whether mind and matter are essentially the same, or essentially different, they are both alike under one and the same law of compulsory causation." [25]

It is likewise utterly incompatible with Calvinism:

> The doctrine of modern Calvinism, as laid down by Jonathan Edwards and the late Dr. Williams, which represents a will absolutely passive, clay in the hands of a potter, destroys all will, takes away its essence and definition, as effectually as in saying—This circle is square—I should deny the figure to be a circle at all. It was in strict consistency, therefore, that these writers supported the Necessitarian scheme, and made the relation of cause and effect the law of the universe, subjecting to its mechanism the moral world no less than the material or physical. It follows that all is nature. Thus, though few writers use the term Spirit more frequently, they in effect deny its existence, and evacuate the term of all its proper meaning. With such a system not the wit of man nor all the theodices ever framed by human ingenuity, before the celebrated Leibnitz, can reconcile the sense of responsibility, nor the fact of the difference in kind between regret and remorse.
>
> (*On Spiritual Religion Indeed*, Aphorism I)

---

not spirit; and *vice versa* of spirit, that which is not comprehended in nature; or in the language of our elder divines, that which transcends nature. But Nature is the term in which we comprehend all things that are representable in the forms of time and space, and subjected to the relations of cause and effect: and the cause of the existence of which, therefore, is to be sought for perpetually in something antecedent."

[25] In Chapter VII of *Biographia Literaria*, composed 1817, Coleridge says that according to Necessitarians " we only fancy, that we act from rational resolves, or prudent motives, or from impulses of anger, love, or generosity. In all these cases the real agent is a *something-nothing-everything*, which does all of which we know, and knows nothing of all that itself does. The existence of an infinite spirit, of an intelligent and holy will, must, on this system, be mere articulate motions of the air."

Yet the reflecting man must admit that his own will is not the only and sufficient determinant of all he is, and all he does. Something must be attributed to the " harmony of the system to which he belongs, and to the pre-established fitness of the objects and agents, known and unknown, that surround him." Moreover, in the world we see everywhere evidences of a unity, which the component parts are so far from explaining, that they necessarily presuppose it as the cause and condition of their existing as those parts; or even of their existing at all. This antecedent unity, or principle, or universal presence, or Spirit, acts " on the will by a predisposing influence from without, as it were, though in a spiritual manner, and without suspending or destroying its freedom." Thus *the Spirit beareth witness with our spirit*—man is a co-partner with the Divine.

Furthermore, this intercommunion suggests the possibility of man's endless progress in the quest of the spirit. " Every state of religious morality, which is not progressive, is dead or retrograde." And " Christianity is not a theory, or a speculation; but a life—not a philosophy of life, but a life and a living process." The law of method and of mental initiative with its principle of progressive transition, developed in *The Friend,* has its highest and ultimate application in the Christian's " ever-progressive, though never-ending " growth in spiritual truth. It is the culmination of what is a universal law of progress, from the lowest order of creation to the highest:

The lowest class of animals or *protozoa*, the *polypi* for instance, have neither brain nor nerves. Their motive powers are all from without. The sun, light, the warmth, the air are their nerves and brain. As life ascends, nerves appear; but still only as the conductors of an external influence; next are seen the knots or ganglions, as so many *foci* of instinctive agency, which imperfectly imitate the yet wanting centre. And now the promise and token of a true individuality are disclosed; . . . the spontaneous rises into the voluntary, and finally after various steps and long ascent, the material and animal means and conditions are prepared for the manifestations of a free will, having its law within itself, and its motive in the law—and thus bound to originate its own acts, not only without, but even against, alien stimulants. That in our present state we have only the dawning of this inward sun (the perfect law of liberty) will sufficiently limit and qualify the preceding position, if only it have been allowed to produce its two-fold consequence—the excitement of hope and the repression of vanity (*Moral and Religious Aphorisms*, xv). . . . . And who that hath watched their ways with an understanding heart, the filial and loyal bee; the home-building, wedded, and divorceless swallow; and above all the manifoldly intelligent ant tribes, with their commonwealths and confederacies, their warriors and miners, the husbandfolk, that fold in their tiny flocks on the honeyed leaf, and the virgin sisters with the holy instincts of maternal love, detached and in selfless purity—and not say to himself, Behold the shadow of approaching humanity, the sun rising from behind, in the kindling morn of creation! Thus all lower natures find their highest good in semblances and seekings of that which is higher and better. All things strive to ascend, and ascend in their striving. And shall man alone stoop?[26] . . . No! it must be a higher good to make you happy. While you labor for any thing below your proper humanity, you seek a happy life in the region of death. Well saith the moral poet—

<p style="text-align:center;">Unless above himself he can
Erect himself, how mean a thing is man!
(<i>Moral and Religious Aphorisms</i>, xxxvi)</p>

What is peculiar to man, however, and exclusively human, is a struggle of jarring impulses within him; a mysterious diversity between the injunctions of the mind and the elections of the will; an inexplicable sense of moral evil in his nature. The means of redemption from this evil constitutes spiritual religion indeed—something higher than religious morality. This redemption cannot

---

[26] These almost startlingly penetrative passages anticipate, so far as prophecy can anticipate, the evolutionary thought of a later generation, especially on its ethical side, as expressed, for instance, in the poetry of Browning.

be effected merely by a progressive development toward moral perfection, but requires a special revealing and redeeming agency. "I regard," says Coleridge, "the very phrase, 'Revealed Religion,' as a pleonasm, inasmuch as a religion not revealed is, in my judgment, no religion at all." The historic Christ is the Revealer and Redeemer. "I believe Moses, I believe Paul; but I believe in Christ," succinctly expresses Coleridge's meaning. To show that the distinctive principles of Christianity as a redemptive religion are in full accord with right reason and highest conscience is the purpose of the third part of *Aids to Reflection*.

"The two great moments of the Christian Religion are, Original Sin and Redemption." [27] Without a distinct comprehension of the meaning of the term Original Sin it is impossible to understand aright any one of the doctrines peculiar to Christianity. Original sin, then, is "sin originant, underived from without," that is, it is not a thing in nature, where all is Necessity, cause and effect, antecedent and consequent—" in nature there can be no origin." Sin therefore is a spiritual, not a natural, evil; but the spiritual in man is the will; in and by the will sin must originate. It is a thing neither inflicted on man, nor implanted in him, not inherited by him: "For if it be sin, it must be original; and a state or act, that has not its origin in the will, may be calamity, deformity, disease, or mischief; but a sin it can not be." The question, therefore, of the chronology of sin, or the chronicles of the first sinner, or of the supposed connecting links of an adamantine chain from the first sinner down to ourselves, has only

[27] Coleridge considers many other articles of the Creed, such as Election, The Trinity, Baptism, etc., but since these are matters for the Speculative, not the Practical, Reason to consider, they admit of great varieties of opinion without affecting the character of the Christian.

a metaphysical and historical interest; and the question as to whether sin is of God or co-equal with God becomes a barren controversy. What the individual must primarily concern himself with is, not what inherited tendencies or diseases he is afflicted with, but what moral evil he has originated in his own responsible will; for that alone is sin.

Nevertheless, original sin is confessedly a mystery, one which by the nature of the subject must ever remain such, which is felt to be such by every one who has previously convinced himself that he is a responsible being—a mystery which admits of no further explanation than the statement of the fact. It is, however, not a fact and a mystery first introduced and imposed by Christianity, but of universal recognition. It is assumed or implied by every religion that retains the least glimmering of the patriarchal faith in a God infinite, yet personal. A deep sense of this fact is in the most ancient books of the Brahmins; in the Atheism of the Buddhists; in the myths of Prometheus, of Io, and of Cupid and Psyche—" in the assertion of Original Sin the Greek Mythology rose and set." It is as great a perplexity for the philosophic Deist as for the Christian; so that a man may not get rid of the difficulty by ceasing to be a Christian.

It is in the Christian Scriptures alone, however, that original sin is affirmed with the force and frequency proportioned to its consummate importance. And it is the Christ alone of these Scriptures that supplies an adequate redemption from its power. The Redemptive Act is complete and perfect in itself. Christ, sinless, voluntarily took upon himself our humanity; and though his death was violent, he accepted it with an inward willingness of spirit, which was its real cause. The power of sin was conquered by his Spirit. It is not merely by steadfastness of will, or determination, but by *steadfastness in faith,* faith in something higher than the will—the redemptive power of Christ's love—that the will can be saved from the consequences of original sin, that is, be regenerated, and that the self can be emptied of evil and filled with grace and truth.

Redemption is in no sense a credit-debit account between two parties (God and man) into which a third party (Christ) enters to pay the debt to satisfy the creditor. But the Redeemer, by taking on human flesh and conquering sin in the flesh, created a condition by which man may be a co-agent with the Spirit of Christ; and through repentance and faith, the two constantly interacting, and through his will, working in conjunction with both repentance and faith, man may attain to salvation. That is, redemption is a spiritual process and a spiritual mystery. And things spiritual must be apprehended spiritually.

The redemptive experience has a true inwardness and is transcendental. A Christian cannot speak or think as if his redemption were a future or contingent event, but must both feel and say, "I have been redeemed, I am justified." Christ did not merely come to show us a way of life, to teach certain opinions and truths, and tell us of a resurrection; but he declared He is the Way, the Truth, the Resurrection, the Life; God manifested in the flesh is eternity in the form of time. The Absolute Reason in Christ became human reason. And the method of redemption furnishes the means for the human reason to become one with the Absolute Reason, the human will with the Absolute Will. Just as the understanding in man utilizes the material furnished by the senses to its own ends, just as the reason utilizes the understanding to its own and higher ends—just as, in other words, there is an antecedent and higher mental initiative in every act of mental and moral growth—so the Redeemer furnishes the antecedent moral and spiritual initiative to the will that it might free itself, not only of its own original sin, but of ultimate corruption and carnal death, and become free indeed. Thus the method of redemption offered in the Scriptures is in absolute harmony with right reason and highest conscience.

Since the redemptive experience is an inward process of purifying the heart and the will and must needs be had by every Christian, it follows that the question of miracles and the question of immortality are relatively of less importance as attesting the truth of religion. As to miracles, it may freely be admitted and even contended that those worked by Christ were to the whole Jewish nation true and appropriate evidences as to the nature of him who worked them and proof of the truth of his teachings. But what if, as Paley taught, these external and historical data are substituted for the inward experience of religion itself as evidences of Christianity? Coleridge retorts: " Evidences of Christianity! I am weary of the word. Make a man feel the want of it; rouse him, if you can, to the self-knowledge of his need of it; and you may safely trust to its own evidence." Likewise an intellectual assent to belief in immortality, which is a fundamental article of faith in all other religions as well as Christianity, cannot be substituted for the possession of that inward grace and truth which came by Jesus Christ.

In thus setting himself squarely against Jonathan Edwards and Paley and all the Necessitarian and rational theologians of the eighteenth century, and in transfusing religion with imaginative and spiritual insight, Coleridge became a prophet of the nineteenth century and an influential power in philosophy and literature as well as in religion. He not only inveighed mightily against his own early views and all theologies that conceive God as a law of gravitation, and that empty the words sin and holiness of their real meaning, but against all schemes of conduct based on calculations of self-interest. Of such schemes he says:

> They do not belong to moral science, to which, both in kind and purpose, they are in all cases foreign, and, when substituted for it, hostile. Ethics, or the science of Morality, does indeed in no wise exclude the consideration of action; but it contemplates the same in its originating spiritual source, without reference to space or time, or sensible existence. Whatever springs out of *the perfect law of freedom*, which exists only by its unity with the will of God, its inherence in the Word of God, and its communion with the Spirit of God— that (according to the principles of moral science) is good —it is light and righteousness and very truth (*On Spiritual Religion Indeed*, XIII).

This inward spiritual religion postulates a wider transcendence; namely, that in general of the spiritual over the material world, and militates against our habit of attaching all our conceptons and feelings to the objects of the senses: "I do not hesitate to assert, that it was one of the great purposes of Christianity, and included in the process of our redemption, to rouse and emancipate the soul from this debasing slavery to the outward senses, to awaken the mind to the true *criteria* of reality, namely, permanence, power, will manifested in act, and truth operating in life." Indeed, throughout *The Friend* and *Aids to Reflection* Coleridge insists that the visible objects of nature have reality only so far as there is in them a principle of permanence akin to the 'peculia' of humanity, "without which indeed they not only exist in vain, as pictures for moles, but actually do not exist at all;" —one long peroration on the text in *Dejection: An Ode* (1802): "We receive but what we give, and in our life alone does Nature live."

That the presupposition throughout *Aids to Reflection* of faith in God as personal, with moral attributes, and in Christ as more than human, meant something other to Coleridge than a matter of mere intellectual assent is attested by a letter to Stuart, in 1826, which expresses his personal acceptance of faith in God and in a Redeemer and belief in the efficacy of prayer. In consequence he became more cheerful and more resigned than formerly. About this same time he freed himself measurably from the evil of opium; thenceforth he passed his days in the serenity of old age and in the spirit of a personal and transcendental religion.

But a revealed and transcendental religion, based on the Word of God, implies some special method or principle of interpreting the Bible. The question of interpretation Coleridge discusses in a little treatise *Confessions of an Inquiring Spirit,* posthumously published. The cautiousness with which he argues against Infallibility—the theory that the Bible throughout was literally dictated by Omniscience—indicates how universally the theory was held in Coleridge's day; the clearness and boldness with which he presents his own opposing view makes him one of the forerunners of the free and so-called 'higher' criticism of later times.

Coleridge contends that the Bible should be approached in the same spirit that one approaches any other books of grave authority. One may, for instance, consider as un-Shakespearian passages in *Titus Andronicus* and other plays of Shakespeare, and yet speak with absolute certainty concerning the manifold beauties of Shakespeare, both in general and with detail. To deem every line in Shakespeare as authoritative and praiseworthy as every other line would be critical fanaticism. Likewise it is " superstitious and unscriptural " to consider that since the

Bible was dictated by God Himself every word in it is as precious as every other word. In short, it is the spirit of the Bible, and not the detached words and sentences, that is infallible and absolute. And he who "takes it up as he would any other body of ancient writings, the livelier and steadier will be his impression of its superiority to all other books, till at length all other books and all other knowledge will be valuable in his eyes in proportion as they help him to a better understanding of his Bible."

Though Christianity has its historical evidences as strong as is compatible with the nature of history, "the truth revealed through Christ has its evidence in itself, and the proof of its divine authority is its fitness to our nature and needs." For this transcendental or pragmatical test nothing can ever be substituted; the true inwardness of the Scriptures must find response in the true inwardness of man's soul. This Coleridge eloquently expounds in *Notes on the Book of Common Prayer,* where he speaks of preparations for taking the Sacrament of the Eucharist:

Read over and over again (he says) the Gospel according to St. John, till your mind is familiarized to the contemplation of Christ, the Redeemer and Mediator of mankind, yea, of every creature, as the living and self-subsisting Word, the very truth of all true being, and the very being of all enduring truth; the reality, which is the substance and unity of all reality. . . . We are assured, and we believe, that Christ is God; God manifested in the flesh. As God, he must be present entire in every creature;—(for how can God or indeed any spirit, exist in parts?)

This transcendent, monistic, and purely mystical Unity represents the final stage of Coleridge's spiritual development.

In *Religious Musings* of 1794 Coleridge began with the conception of Unity and with an effort to harmonize whatever light he possessed with the Scriptures; these two factors therefore are common to all the stages of his religious development. Thus Unity is both the most constant and the most important principle in his religious philosophy, while the Bible, in which St. John plays a special part, is the most important influence in shaping that philosophy. On the other hand, the widest divergence in his thought is this, that whereas in the first stage he represented Deity as impersonal and "not only as a necessary but a necessitated being," man as an automaton "predoomed" to a fixed course, and all things in the universe as regulated into a necessary universal harmony, in the second stage he gradually emancipated himself from this conception and became transcendental, conceiving God as personal [28] and self-determined, and man as having conscience and free-will and other transcendent qualities, by means of which he is able to effect a higher Unity with the power and Will of God. Though this divergence involves a complete facing about on a fundamental issue, Coleridge's religious writings, when studied in chronological order, show a consistent growth, beginning with a thorough-going Necessitarianism and ending in a radical Transcendentalism. They were one of the most important influences in changing the current of English thought from characteristic eighteenth-century determinism and Necessitarianism to characteristic nineteenth-century Idealism.

S. F. GINGERICH.

[28] Of his transition period Coleridge writes in *Biographia Literaria* (Chapter x): "For a very long time, indeed, I could not reconcile personality with infinity: and my head was with Spinoza, though my whole heart remained with Paul and John. Yet there had dawned upon me, even before I had met with the *Critique of Pure Reason*, a certain guiding light. . . . I became convinced, that religion, as both the corner-stone and the key-stone of morality, must have a moral origin; so far at least, that the evidence of its doctrines could not, like the truths of abstract science, be wholly independent of the will."

MARQUETTE UNIVERSITY LIBRARIES
MEM. 828.7C67zG5
From necessity to transcendentalism in C

3 5039 00028718 2

Date Due

DEMCO NO. 38-300